The National Poetry Series was establi~~~~~~~~~~~~~~
publication of five poetry books annually through five participating
publishers. Publication is funded by the Lannan Foundation,
Stephen Graham, the Joyce & Seward Johnson Foundation,
Glenn and Renee Schaeffer, and Juliet Lea Hillman Simon~~

2009 COMPETITION

Julie Carr of Denver, Colorado, *Sarah—Of Fragments and Lines*
Chosen by Eileen Myles, published by Coffee House Press

Colin Cheney of Brooklyn, New York, *Here Be Monsters*
Chosen by David Wojahn, published by University of Georgia Press

Carrie Fountain of Austin, Texas, *Burn Lake*
Chosen by Natasha Trethewey, published by Penguin Books

Erika Meitner of Blacksburg, Virginia, *Ideal Cities*
Chosen by Paul Guest, published by HarperCollins Publishers

Jena Osman of Philadelphia, Pennsylvania, *The Network*
Chosen by Prageeta Sharma, published by Fence Books

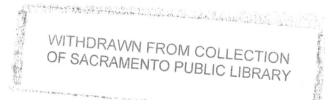
SARAH—OF FRAGMENTS AND LINES

POEMS

JULIE CARR

COFFEE HOUSE PRESS

MINNEAPOLIS

2010

Coffee House Press books are available to the trade through our primary distributor, Consortium Book Sales & Distribution, www.cbsd.com or (800) 283-3572. For personal orders, catalogs, or other information, write to: info@coffeehousepress.org.

Coffee House Press is a nonprofit literary publishing house. Support from private foundations, corporate giving programs, government programs, and generous individuals helps make the publication of our books possible. We gratefully acknowledge their support in detail in the back of this book.

To you and our many readers around the world,
we send our thanks for your continuing support.

LIBRARY OF CONGRESS CIP INFORMATION

Carr, Julie
Sarah; of fragments and lines : poems / by Julie Carr.
p. cm.
ISBN 978-1-56689-251-3 (alk. paper)
I. Title.
PS3603.A77425S27 2010
811'.6—dc22
2010018655

PRINTED IN THE UNITED STATES
1 3 5 7 9 8 6 4 2
FIRST EDITION | FIRST PRINTING

Thank you to Noah Eli Gordon, Joseph Lease, Rusty Morrison, Evelyn Reilly, Margaret Ronda, and Andrew Zawacki for friendship and for reading. Thanks to Linda Norton for her artwork and for continued guidance and inspiration. My gratitude to Eileen Myles for selecting this book. And finally, love and gratitude to Tim Roberts.

ACKNOWLEDGMENTS

Berkeley Poetry Review: "In the second week of solid rain . . . "; *Boston Review:* "Grief Abstracts"; *Copper Nickel:* "Lines for what is Broken," "Bird Fragments" (Quail can't see), "Bird Fragments" (Coos in the dust), "Supposition Poem"; *The Nation:* "Four-Syllable Lines (Monody)"; *New American Writing:* "Landlocked Lines," "Self-Loathing Lines"; *Octopus:* "Daylight Abstracts," "Waiting Abstracts," "Conception Abstracts," "Fear Fragments," "Sudden Fragment: Home," "Motherless Abstracts," "Lines of Defense"; *Palimpsest:* "Lines for the Wind," "Death Fragment" (Furrows of ash), "Death Fragments" (Smudged water glass); *Parthenon West:* "Lines for a Storm," "Lines for Revision"; *A Public Space:* "Lines of Refusal"; *Puerto del Sol:* "Conception Fragment," "Fragments for Linda," "Of Sarah" (Decay to the lemon); *Women's Studies Quarterly:* "Metaphor Poem"

*For Margaret Ronda
and Carolyn Grace*

Landlocked Lines

There were people behind closed doors, people on the other side

A specter haunting now hidden now fled

Under the firmament above the firmament and so on

Plastic cup, plastic tooth, nipple, phone, call me

I was filming a movie but my brother took my camera and broke it

Then he fell on his face and laughed into the snow

Zebra and xylophone cyclone and sorrow

Before they lay down, the men of the city circled the park

Circled the park circled the park the park the park

Stood before the door holding the wrapped infant and

I was writing a poem in the alley, a woman came, hovered near, asked for my pen, I gave it up

Consumed in inequity, consumed: give me a child or I will
die, she said

Shrugs away our hands, our mother in the bath in the garden

The music is not great because she said because of the
sadness she said

Primate and psyche umbrage and rag

It can refer only to itself or to the objects that surround it:
lamp, table

It would be absurd to imagine the absent person in the
margins of the book

Red couch, red wall behind

The birds are inside the trees now the first one and the
second one

Giraffe and guest honor and hunt

Then she gave up her spirit but couldn't get out

Daylight Abstracts

Now flare. Now come to this. Now speaking of
plastics, salt, snow.

Bright maybe, I cannot give up on you. Can't taste now
or rare or last. Snow's got its own flash of rightness, own
door to, say, plow or slung or sky of gunmetal floating
down. Said on rising, walking: can't love this ordinary
diurnal run? Can't not.

Always presenting: Own doors, own chairs, roads, ads.
Am I in the wrong place now? Snow's laced by exhaust.
Don't own sex or house just ringed by, walled in. Haul
my rude ways to righteous? Night? I've ruined its
effervescent waves.

Now flight, now gift, now speaking of plastics, of
rapture of rise. Woke corridored by calendar, woke
exhausted in face, spoken of and speaking into thing cold
and needing. Needling too.

Old darkness ruptured, old bent over defeated,

now rectangles of fluorescent, of bold blonde daylight
on walls of old dreck now shine like gestalt or defense,
like splayed hair. Now old odes or seeds of thought
turned snug in gummy mugs: I'm alone here in a day
like an arrow or a lance in a gash. Day, don't say things,
don't order,

don't bend me, don't mold.

Wheel

Sometimes beaches
blend their salt with
ketchup and tin

Hit by Floridian
sun the women turn
to rubber wombing

I'm all that: all that
tin and sugar
salting the eye

Sons and daughters
upward dragged
in cages on a wheel

lips pressed and
knuckled

hands, adult-longing leaking through
bare shoulders in the bright

—again, brighter

Far below:
the flooded loaded
shore

Lines for the New Year

Consider the light, how it offers itself. To the roofs, to snow
    as done-for as a shoelace in a dog's mouth, to the best of
    best of best

Of parties of conspiracy theorists—carrot spears and spooning—it
might come to this. Is this

No one respects especially or much. Not. Cousins on a couch, arms
    of the king of anguish, extended

And what is it you're trying to tell me with your locked eyes?

Simmer and miser and rise

It's my throat you're kissing, your hard-on, or whatever to add to
    my cup

Foamed and fingered and free

An election year. O. Dust mites spin on guilt-ridden heat. Dire guilt.
What's an eye spot? An eye-sore, a
                    sunspot, piss pot

A new?

I'm ready to cannibalize my own past. Must mean I've no love for
    myself or for narrative

Skating's a dumb circular joy. Hi! More sweet cake, wet ache, weak hate

Could I eat a tree?

Dad's new girlfriend's fur and lips in salmon, tangerine, egg white,
        walls

Forgot to say good-bye to her

The Cuban singer's vacant spouse watches TV in the Home

Word "home"'s got sickening mouth-feel like backing into a sooty
ice bank

Lock-eye, stop staring. Do you expect me to help you locate yourself?

What's on the other side of that hedge? Consider the hedge. O. Take me

To the pool. The spigot, pig's gut, parrot rot: This kind of readymade
        know-how gets you nowhere
        but

That's better than all your

Stories set in funerals and airplanes
together

Conception Fragment

daylight and tree buds

                                petro-

detritus and dust

                               what's winged

in the open   of your pregnancy?

Consider the weight of the face, the river at six,
at seven.

Safe and safer, in courtyards and carpets she's semblance
of balance—what *was* her. Said the lipstick and wig: Go
walk with that chill in your mouth. Go talking on cells
and on landlines. Go empty the pan and the pen.
Empty at six and empty at seven, bed is at eight and
darkness at nine. Empty at waking and empty at
walking. A sheet of shade under that van. A sheet of
shade and a buildup of calling, a bigger buildup of cells.

Consider the exit, the exit 19: it's trees till it's cables,
then Applebee's and babies. Comes cupped in paper,
my upper, my intake, I'm often exhausted in stores.

What's drifting or drinking in rivers looks oily—

the quivery light of the sun. I'm speaking of mouths, of
chairs, meds, laps. Of Bibles and plush and bile and

bills. Like nothing that comes from the cry in the wall, like nothing the ghost out the side of my head. A woman who hangs with Biblical figures can't speed her departure, her anger's still firm. Piled up bedclothes; it looks like they lost one; there's nothing but waiting, there's nothing but waiting, there's nothing but waiting and meals.

Waiting Fragments

Fluorescent exit hangs midair   mid country

    Chandelier flash   on

    machine snow

Meadow, door, this glass

        evaporates: girl pouring in

      drifting confetti

    —

Chimes of thirst

the number nine on the screen—nine barns, nine malls—
a covering haze—

    Food drives in the foothills, an airless winter

chalk on my shirt

      wormholes in the remnants of a dead tree

      The archivist whirls the unfurling losses

Lines for what is Broken

Eyes downward and the bowl slipped from the table (the human's

Need for milk for grain the malleable brain what drugs do—sedate block

Stabilize *philosophy begins when one stops trying to describe things*

You said like a carny from the amusement park a few oats a jumble of

Raincoats husband's turned face call of an owl the things one chooses

Not to describe the curled edges of a book jacket the sweat sliding

Along a boy's jaw the mind damaged repeating *not for me not for me*

The mind in fear plays games of extension as when

A novelist writes of the Manchurian Incident history book on the desk

Before him his enthusiasm far less than when he describes again

Sexual arousal sexual release in the book only occasionally

Does a woman need animalistically the body of another to enter her

Change her *It was not his body but his body's desire for me that made me*

Want to use him as a tool for breaking open what I had begun to

Construct she says just as the grief you are recording can suddenly seem

Too limited too circumscribed you must find a way to tear its

skin) then hit the floor

Western Wind: An Ode

One's mother's brain's
like one of those egg sacs

that lists by slack waves of seaweed and gull-prints—
still speaking abundance—found washed up to rotting

wood of a trap

Trees without leaves and dogs without leashes
simmering wheels of company cars

The body's a hole through which other bodies move

Of Sarah

Years having passed, the foliage is wet: the final morning on which you, in freedom, lie awake. I see your entrapment as a fault of my own, my failure to house you in my own face.

A girl we know has memorized the witches' song. Her serious mouth, unbrushed hair hiding black eyes: Fillet-of-a-fenny-snake-in-the-cauldron-boil-and-bake-eye-of-newt-and-toe-of-frog-wool-of-bat-and-tongue-of-dog. No pause, no breath, as if forced as if always as if gripped.

And you, ungripped, have been trained to know less. The training arduous, lasting for ages—your entire lifetime. First you had to give up the meaning of words. And then water.

Death Fragment

Furrows of ash and

surge of a voice

Two messages: the first—your mother is dead

The second—your mother is not dead

The heartbeat gallops

into our room

Conception Abstracts

Heat teems from the meat of the form.

Tame heat if tame form, if maimed form then fierce.
Seems eaten, this mate, this timed tenant.

Tenured member of my own passive nature, I tested the tine of the task. Desperate for some apt rapture, tapped the lap of the master. Faster. Water and laughter, the last splatter of summer, later, the hot slap of not sleeping. Walled by fault, the taut self slipped. And to what heights after?

City Gravity Fragments

Verily beat

    under wrap of blue blue

stuttery

                brick and glass tongues

     —

Between banks and   dead-end training for plunderers

       skylines like silk

bras for businesses:

           palindromes with sustenance sucked

out: desks, sills, turnstiles, I'm late

       to this ecology

and I can't get out

          its rhythm's so

                  metro

nymic

Fear Fragments

rodent in the fir tree

in the

alphabet and telephone: fur

Rodent—from *gnaw*

and scratch she can't—now

speak can't, now, see—

—

In the blood of the infant

a something that

forgets   erodes: from *rodent* the

not

knowable the
gnathic

ungathered as a carcass

of a left-by car

Pregnancy Abstracts

Slack as the cigarette smoker slouched in his seat then taut as a show tune turned toward closure. Lacks no louche motive, she's lavish in her secure culture. No longer just cluster, now tasting future. Wamble or stumble not, not in that locked sea she walks in.

Now I see a face. Sea then snow then ice.

Surface of salt, something like sky, like froth at the flat of the shore. It gathers and leaves and gathers and leaves. What is is sure but only in-known.

Weighted foliage and kicking heel. Soon the bakery opens. My liege, I am tired, already on waking in the rain. Every boy with a stick, every ache of the pen, every fool's me. The split or slit of me's unseared, unsutured. This being's strut rests not. Veil of rain in the leaves again. Tangle of future untried, untied. To gain's my ruse, my reason, my route. Gnast's a spark, a bit of coming, a flit or flash in the foot of it.

Bird Fragments

Quail can't see, caught and bound
She, mistress,
died crystalline with echoes of lead

Quail gives feast
of id; her core of nuance, her

sonorous state,
stilled

Come in little avian baby
A safe universe
only in arms—

—

Under cover of evening
a waterfall goes
the color of sex

Smoked in the odors of grill and mud

tender dove, tremulous and bare

Of Sarah

Decay to the lemon. To the crust of bread. But not to the dog that leaps against the door, not to its owner in camouflage, his lank hair and heavy glasses. Decay, Sarah, also far from you, your place in the trees—the way their fullness makes the landscape three-dimensional now, almost June. That green before green before green, that roundness we perceive as the air—this is your roundness, your green.

As a child on the boardwalk you seemed patient, contemplative. In fact, you were angry and for good cause. Then, your anger turned quiet. Now it peels from the throats of birds: rage in song.

But when I sleep your face remains placid: the face of all women who were not my mother but who I imagined as my mother. Wander through.

Sarah: Prosopopoeia

"I lost the words for what I most cared about until uncaring I fell asleep in a chair and waking walked one shoe on one shoe off holding a hand but whose seeing out a window but what and no one could find my other."

Four-Syllable Lines (Monody)

Sweet unrest still

Wood harsh dismal

Slope of a hill

Darkening air

She's the target

Force-drift and thrown

Dismissed rash tear

I would, can, did

Slip in a hole

Now stab butt out

Doting body

Been thrown below

She's the it girl

Her epic dust

Sudden Fragment: Home

This life without animals without rain

Dry air from behind a crest like a hawk

This without bridges without sand

or a heron with no face—

Such is sudden

is remote

Grief Abstracts

Flit and click of the clock. Rim of my wrist
in the sum of the light.

By which I. By which. Trill of bird, answer. As might.

A word turns in a thought while a foot's in the, the literate
belly: timed, measured, kissed.

Mired in rhyme, I rise and am two. A ruse or a wraith.
Doubled, I see so. See the hedge of the sky with the edge
of my eye. The face of my kind with my mind.

The doubled woman is a common thing. Nothing more
common than this, this slide of myself from one to two to
none. Something to something more to nothing then. And
the nothing that my maker becomes contains me as the
space does a bit of air. Flawlessly and firm.

Grief of fire in its final flash and smolder.
The weight of her speaks spark's brief ire become ash,

become ruinous food full of dolor. To recall her
laughter is to grow older. Fear's rife in this filial order.
If molded, I'm fodder for air, and I'm colder. Since I
lost her I stored her like ore in my form as if later I'd
find her, restore her.

Slow and ready-rising, grief draws similes. Slides over
for intrusions of likeness: berry bush, clay, beaded wire,
bread torn for toddler. Bored grief wards a rose bloom
by the door. Gravity suffices as thought. Thought's
grafted or scratched, as a plant or a lens. Sad thought,
assiduous in its pursuits, beating devotion into the
body, as a small and forced wary focus.

Supposition Poem

If silent at four the couch
If the book in my hand allows sleep
Like another hand I am holding
If she bears no resemblance to herself
As we knew her as she knew herself
Wearing a resemblance, a semblance, of the self
If dressed in the body of another
If feeding
If wearing this baby as I wear my face
If I become undressed of myself
If on the couch reading or sleeping
A figure, a shape, some matter
The red couch and the red wall behind it
At the wire waking
If another's pain ever travels
If another's pleasure
If weight of the body on the couch
Weight of the body on the couch
If eating is feeding another, if eating is denying another
If dressed in the silence of being never another
If wearing the baby and also my face and the cloth that is the silence
            of not hearing, not being able to hear, another
If the window is the sign of departure, the eventual departure
            from all others

If the soul is in the body a silence
The silence of flames that don't sputter don't burn out
The red couch and the red wall behind
If the book is as close to another as ever—
      wearing the baby and face
      wall behind

Futurity Fragments

Her naked form in the dream
submerged in three inches of water

Laughter—her laughter   a kind of

                    lye in which she

bathes

      —

        Now for the movement of trash cans and trains
        for they, like one's self,

vessels for

      some other life

Self-Loathing Lines

There was nothing left but the lantern, the palisade, and the sky

Someone knocks. It's her soft spot, a self-taught store-bought

Hotty. Rain stops. I'm busy on bluish earth the laptop running ill

First she bent over to tie her shoe then she tore her rent check up

Nothing left but the breast pump the blanket the slow blink of her

Darkness like a foraging hand stilled the crying stole the branches and

The imaged aged inner body

Away

Insert: Detail Given

Illness arrived first in the head. Felt in the eyes as a film. A pillaged language—the blank of seeing, then saying, less. A dog appeared and we could read that sound. Daughter sighed in her bed. The boy whistled and we silenced him. Chirp of a bird we could do nothing to suppress. The buoyancy of children and animals, of their mouths and eyes, must somehow be quelled if we are to live. Tried to bite until the restraints. Streams of swearing: not even the professionals could. Nor should they? Who then? To give a person up, to give up *on* the person. To wait simply or to hope less simply for her to give, over.

Sucked tongue, mother's scarf, the overripe berries spill. Benched in the heat, kids eat cake, pigeons without feet.

But not needing one, sulkily I am one. Not needing one, sulkily, I am. Some sounds have no origin. Some flowers need no sun. Well cover with weeds surrounding, the hand cutting apples, keying words.

Seated in a sash of light, read: "Someone has combed her hair, has ironed her clothes for school." I'm trained by the lash of the known, in crowds of farmish or suburban homes, where the craving for solitude is not satisfied by solitude, for company not satisfied by others.

Speech not by speaking. Sleep never by sleep.

Pregnancy Fragments

cave, the Greek word *kyma*:
swell, wave, cabbage sprout

where locate?

the actual

—

to replace tension with

attention—but to what?

Objects arranged synchronically

beginning with foot, then match, then

a photo of the countryside

Ignoring antecedents

at the same time entirely bound by

To enter or to inter.

Both rely on the earth. Terra: which in turn rests on thirst. The earth's opening up: a sigh in the dirt and it *will* turn. As one enters the other is interred. The wet who comes in, but from within. The very dry one who goes out by going in. I am sorry, which is to say sore, or full of sorrow. To rely is to rally or to re-tie, to gather. This ligamental terrain we lie on. In.

Think of the old, the destroyed. I was a king. Now given as food. Which is an honor. To be eaten. To expect, at the table, a reprisal. Of myself.

The torn bit of skin is expectant: waits to be replaced.

I'm placed as kin toward word. Guarding and regarding that which will round or will rend me.

Knead this matter, this measured month. From kneading comes making: the entwining of mass. If needed I am rounded, insinuated, now sinuous. Mass around which I, curved, imply or am implied. For which and by which I am transparent.

Leapt

Caught a fish breaking water to what unmakes her

Diagnosed by the air: out and triggered

Weary and bound what thought sucked

Bound bound

And we kissed her

in the safety of the public bulb light

In the second week of solid rain, Sarah. You wake at dawn with a head of dream. Clover's fell enthusiasm expands in the perpetual bath. Sarah. The lamp suspended in the garden, Sarah: Cheshire-like and falsely dear. We make boats of juice bottles, houses of cereal boxes, cats of toilet paper, eggs of lavender and stone. Sarah. At the festival of water we watch an orchestra of children sway to the music of their strings. And in your room you succumb. Learn as you are dying how to behave like one near dead. As magpie, you are eave-bound, acquisitive, indiscriminate. Beak clipping the scraps of your old existence, the strings of your future weave, Sarah. As duck you are industrious, with a reed in your possession, across pond you slide. But here, tatter-head, you are forced into days, broken into hours, and those hours mercilessly sliced.

Lines for Revision

There were people behind closed doors, people on the other side

The cop on his motorcycle tailing me

His parents invented a language, wrote a book in that language, and named him after the main character

I was not suspicious of the couple buying children's books until someone pointed out that they did not have a child

Two men in the park admired my baby: "How old, how old?" Then, "That's one of those meaning-of-the-universe type things"

The tree jumped into itself and remained, framed and hung

Boys hurled wads of dirt at one another while the Wicca group completed their ritual: Little girls in velvet gowns: "Food time!"

The woman on the phone, her dog in her lap: "Who can remember these things?" or the waists of men?

Broken stumps scavenge the sky

Willows whiten, aspen quiver. The Viennese scholar of the avant-garde swallows his tea as the baby wakes in the Shakespeare garden

Night: A stranger among humans (Hölderlin)

Whether one can feel the news as one can feel one's own hands.
Whether one can feel one's own hands as one feels the news

What else can words do? I'm no closer to her without them

She hesitates before the train, while under the tree, the former mayor of
the former city

What is the music of that line? This book is your mother and your father.
How it walks all over you

Sarah

Then the quarry where I learned to swim. How you watched me from the ledge as I suddenly, illogically, stopped moving my limbs.

Lapping up water, the cat masters its survival.

Bottle-fed once a lamb in my lap. The sucking more focused than any one noun or stone. To position myself between such need and its fulfillment seemed then the most honorable of seats. But now I find I cannot, with any steadiness, sit there.

But perhaps this never happened? Just as you were never a woman who birthed me.

And stilled the clouds.

Metaphor Poem

Bits of food on the floor—abundance and decay
The removal of a lens cap is history and is memory loss
Weedy lawn means rain's exuberance and no companion
The tear in her skin means sugar
The tear in her skin is a sleepless night, a hard commute, a broken zipper
News of a bombing and a locked museum, blood in an infant's veins
Excess is a streaming ribbon or a streaming ribbon a song
A distant cloud is the perfection of the present and a mark of inattention
The end of the honey is one's mother's death and is one's mother
A boy's curved shoulder, a twelve-foot crater
Where once was a town center
A bottle of water is order in the capital
Ink is her face and is her sleepless night
A streaming ribbon, the end of the honey
A distant cloud—a lens cap removed
A bit of food on the floor of her thought

Exhaustion Fragment

White curtains hang ceiling to floor

motionless   To

feel one's face as

white curtains hanging ceiling to—

Bird Fragments

Coos in the dust of unwashed

rare earth, avid

Avers like one I was, like

the veriest fool alive

—

Aural being. Chirr.

Avian but craven

did, enervated, fall.

Gathered as hole as

pure sound then pure

letter: Written into

dirt.

Death Fragments

smudged water glass

    as refusal

   no photo of the face could

        resume

her seat by the door

   —

the inner part of a bowl of olives gives back the window glance

torn edge of a bag of tomatoes reveals the purposeful hand

weight of the eyelid, press of the lips, charged with living want

wheels of a cart and squeal of a pup do not, will not, carry

no ferry

Lines of Defense

Their own sense of failure is what makes them so mean

Pale blue, heavy leaves, power lines, slept with baby

Constant companion: the air

Problem with that

Corrosives in the pool, new wood in that floor: problem with that too

A bush talking through me, but is it a real bush? Let's check

What is boredom? I tire of I
                    of Garden Center and trips to the bathroom

Close to Home: The Ice Pops: Summer Duck: Sharky

To sleep on the phantom's knee, to wake too early to fantasies of
                    sun on flower, sun on grass. Sufficient?

Day-thoughts: honey, body cream, salt. Wax, fingerprint, bloom over
          bloom

Agrarian longing of fatted cows

With that, with that, a problem

Vodka in their water bottles, so we had to ban the water bottles
      Knives in the pockets, so we had to ban pockets

Nothing so sweet as an ankle in straps, nothing so heirloom as soda and chips

New guidelines, new stats, new bodies of boys: sorry for that, for those

Fast Jack: Luster King: Low Rent: The Hope

Blind Ambition: Max X: Huber: Blood Cow

Nothing so sure as the top of a tree, nothing so hard as abandoned devotion

As the word "force," the word "ok," the words "drift" and "away"

Sarah

I was a bird. A bird in a play and my first line was "bird." There, at the window, another bird, a real one. Dutifully theatrical, I learned to fly by leaping from the ledge, running in the grass. When it was time to come inside, you bathed me in the sink, pouring water over my head.

Yesterday in the queen's channel we rowed a boat aimlessly under sun. A boy about eleven with thin struggling arms also rowed a boat, his grandmother seated before him. Her smile was shy if only because her admiration so intense. The word comes from Latin, *intendĕre,* to stretch out, and now, like so many things, seems to have reversed its meaning. Our intensities are small, wound up and relentless, balls made of rubber, hurled.

In the book I am reading a man has lost his father. Lost him to death, but lost him before that to death-in-life: his father's refusal to live among others. When I became a bird, it was precisely because, dressed in feathers, I could hop and dart about with friends. Not to be alone, to be among. In the other book I am reading, a child in a war is lost to her parents, sent to live in a foreign city where she, to survive, learns to speak to the birds.

The grandmother was in fact stretched out: her bare shins before her, her back against the backrest, her face tilted toward the sun, toward the boy, there, in the queen's channel, in which we, also, rowed.

And you, absolved, the depth into which, the oars, upon which, the birds.

Lines for the Wind

But that was all

the rest could not

penetrate

I entirely

impervious to

bland uneager seductions so why

anyway speak daughter breakfast

snow these nouns

of the normal not say oil not

warming. In L.A. someone took a free tree

didn't plant it

someone

planted but didn't

water

—

To write is audacious

Heat on but I don't want to warm a mouse

feed a child

A woman went into the woods and buried herself standing, only her head remained in the air like a flower

Had to bend down to feed her I suppose

I cannot get the mouse out from under the stove unless I remove the stove, ruin the house

To write in order to leave, for good, the day

There's a dumpster in the back and I can throw my chair into it, my pots and papers, I can

throw my makeup in there

Someone threw a child in and they found her. I cannot throw the floors in, can I?

Speaking and breathing at the level of the foot

When the dumpster is full, someone comes to empty it. I don't have to empty it, but I can get into it

The baby's awake and no one will get her, didn't want to write that, did

My fingernail is split. Been that way for years. Is this split a weapon and can I use it?

For good

Birthday Fragments for Alice

If like a bird, then also like the upward breeze
And if the paper bird is like cream in the spoon,

and the girl like a bird makes patterns in the air,
she's cream also because wanted, and is the spoon's bowl

for the way she holds herself open, but not flatly so,
not unfolded

—

To save her own life, she drew pictures of the witch,
granting the witch *her* wish: to be immortal

To save her own life, she turned a garden to gold
by drawing the witch's eye to the sunlight already shining

Her parents were helpless, having promised her away,
but she was not helpless, not at all

Sarah

And why such a loud voice? Leaning against a parked car, your head under the hood of your jacket. To quiet you is to encourage you. You never could sit alone quietly, play by yourself. And each interaction still a display, a show for the benefit of some other. Even in your best moods you needed this more-than-attention, this wrapping by others as if a match head by a flame. I shushed the other girl. She looked up, surprised.

A friend whose mother is likely dying from cancer in England spends every day with her mother in the hospital. Nine hours a day for as many weeks. One weekend her boyfriend comes to visit. They take a short trip to Dublin. After he leaves and she returns to her routine—riding the bus to the hospital each morning, staying until night, riding the bus back to the small house in the village, walking the dogs, checking her e-mail, going to bed—my friend counts the days until her period is due. Then she is late. Then she is nine days late. This possibility that she might be pregnant begins to pulse inside her head. The idea, which she knows to be illogic, but cannot let go of, is that if she is pregnant the baby will keep her mother alive.

It was 3:56. My eyes blinking to the rhythm of your voice. Who,

I thought, am I pregnant with? For perhaps the baby, shifting under my rib, perhaps this is you? The final thing I said before sleep: "What kind of person is this?" Air in the curtains and sunlight through the glass.

Fragments for Linda

As mosses shore holes

        tendentious hold on

        their dirt, she

tending to open her own store

    to un

        hoard to

raid her own arousal for its

skin

      —

She and she and she is

      needed   sweat eat soup almost

      sleep needed   itch near the

computer

—

Linda don't

stop there   I'd gather you in

pools in stray chairs in

gardens of mosses don't

stop there   your white

sickle shaped   underfoot

to kiss

Lamp. Kicked from the end table.

One symptom after another. Symptoms like licks of
cream precise and paraded. People in chairs who
cannot stand. People with mouths who can no longer
speak. A symptom is a sample tomb or a sign of torn,
a slick luck, sliding.

My hand on the head of the growing thing. Stop. Even
time can break. Odd time's already so or it's stunted.
Sometimes what's growing's not health but tainted. Ink
in a pool at my—

The air that becomes what was. A hand, a head, a knee,
a spine. Now figure for no future. Can break like water
not reforming but fled.

The moveable heart has a place in the face. Has a place
on the sleeve but hollow. The heavy heart falls to the
foot like the lure of lead. To gather the body into a
sleeping weight in a chair means for now no rupture,
just a steady giving downward. That is the broken
thing that, because broken, won't without being
handled rise again. Folded.

Lines of Refusal

Nothing here, just the sound of the heat, the sound of the cars,
nothing, nothing

Sweet unrest

To the oldest son a scythe, to the second a cock, to the third a cat

Must avoid rivers, strivers, and voyeurs

Not gather, not tether, not tie

The young brother came to a town that was completely hung
with black crepe

Wrote his autobiography in exactly thirty-seven words

Crawled into a crawlspace and pulled shut the door

No friend, no grammar, no end

Later, he too will become an imposing statue

No wish, no fission, no sign

Then hurrying across the avenue

Snow and so on

A young red fox and so on

Face and hair and hands and so on

Each with the incomparable taste of its own life in its mouth

Dream Fragment

In a theater the family fills two rows

On the stage another family sits to eat

Behind them on the wall a third family, filmed,

    also sits to eat

"How do we know when something is happening?" she asks

Waiting Fragments

The diapered cat, set sideways on the couch.

Squirrels charged with

furor. Days that are

counted. Tense green of

a leaf. A mind stills to ready.

Itself for.

—

My hands itch, my feet also

"Since nothing involving life comes to that quietness . . ."

A pen becomes

slush or lash of sea

Sun's panic fouls the day, folds the yellow pansy down

Of Sarah Again

Fell asleep in a rowboat, head on your mother's thigh. When you opened your eyes you were in a wider sea and the sun was red into the waves. You were cold, and your mother's hand on your shoulder warmed only that bit of you. If only her hand were larger. The man at the oars was not your father and you didn't know when you'd get to the shore again. Looked for your face in the face of a spoon and found yourself sadly reversed and elongated. So much so now.

Lines for a Storm

So he plucked out his feathers, went and sat by a tradesman's shop, and wept.

With the sunflower nodding and the sirens on steady, she wakes to answer the phone.

Kissing the deck with superstitious ardor, the hand with his cap on is filmed.

And he walked the globe with feet of lead, and she in a window of dust.

Pale blue lines between banks of dark cloud had no choice but to become America.

Wept and wailed until he lost his senses—when the cook came by he gave her pepper when she asked for salt, wheat when she asked for rice.

Two thousand soldiers in the Union army suffering from nostalgia.

And though many of the afflicted were hospitalized, the most serious cases were allowed to return home.

Running as ocean-froth or cloud-wisp in storm-wind, a memory of her small lap her salt scent her blue beads and her eye, blinking.

Parents, advised to train their children to master their emotions, sent them from home so they might grow accustomed to movement and loss.

And she, in this torrent, dissolves.

Lines to Scatter

A perfectly themeless piece of language, fallow in the lap of the wave,
was love like a lemon does, silent, self-charged, struck with sun

*

Buses move by, bass line steadies, the biker's heartbeat secure

*

Some fly or rat, some untoward creature, peeling the wrappers in the
rank dark wakes us

*

Our bet is with the wind—in the wind—of wind, ripped

*

Without memory there's no appearance of now, no way or where for
now to emerge. No

government no travel

*

A dog on the Metro, muzzled

*

"And they, destined to shine like the brightness of the firmament for
ever and ever, they . . ."

Notes

"Landlocked Lines": "A specter haunting now hidden now fled" is from *The Communist Manifesto*.

"Lines for what's Broken": "Philosophy begins when one stops trying to describe things" is from Gertrude Stein.

"Pregnancy Abstracts": The word "gnast" is Old English for "spark."

"Self-Loathing Lines": "There was nothing left but the lamp, the palisade, and the sky" is from Sartre.

"Motherless Abstracts": "Someone has combed her hair, has ironed her clothes for school" is from Paul Hoover.

"Leapt" is a rewrite of Blake's "Infant Sorrow."

"Lines of Defense": "Close to Home," "The Ice Pops," "Summer Duck," "Sharky," "Fast Jack," "Luster King," "Low Rent," "The Hope," "Blind Ambition," "Max X," "Huber," and "Blood Cow" are all names of bands playing in Boston in the summer of 2008.

"Lines of Refusal": The italicized lines are, slightly altered, from Simone de Beauvoir.

"Waiting Fragments": "Since nothing involving life comes to that quietness . . ." is from Nguyen Trai.

"Lines to Scatter": "And they, destined to shine . . ." is, slightly altered, from Daniel 12:3.

THE COFFEE HOUSES of seventeenth-century England were places of fellowship where ideas could be freely exchanged. In the cafés of Paris in the early years of the twentieth century, the surrealist, cubist, and dada art movements began. The coffee houses of 1950s America provided refuge and tremendous literary energy. Today, coffee house culture abounds at corner shops and online.

Coffee House Press continues these rich traditions. We envision all our authors and all our readers—be they in their living room chairs, at the beach, or in their beds—joining us around an ever-expandable table, drinking coffee and telling tales. And in the process of this exchange of stories by writers who speak from many communities and cultures, the American mosaic becomes reinvented, and reinvigorated.

We invite you to join us in our effort to welcome new readers to our table, and to the tales told in the pages of Coffee House Press books.

Please visit www.coffeehousepress.org
for more information.

Funder Acknowledgments

Coffee House Press is an independent nonprofit literary publisher. Our books are made possible through the generous support of grants and gifts from many foundations, corporate giving programs, state and federal support, and through donations from individuals who believe in the transformational power of literature. This book received special support from the National Poetry Series. Coffee House Press receives major operating support from the Bush Foundation, the McKnight Foundation, from Target, and from the Minnesota State Arts Board, through an appropriation from the Minnesota State Legislature and from the National Endowment for the Arts. Coffee House also receives support from: three anonymous donors; Abraham Associates; Allan Appel; Around Town Literary Media Guides; Bill Berkson; the James L. and Nancy J. Bildner Foundation; the Patrick and Aimee Butler Family Foundation; the Buuck Family Foundation; Dorsey & Whitney, LLP; Fredrikson & Byron, P.A.; Jennifer Haugh; Anselm Hollo and Jane Dalrymple-Hollo; Jeffrey Hom; Stephen and Isabel Keating; Robert and Margaret Kinney; the Kenneth Koch Literary Estate; Allan & Cinda Kornblum; the Lenfestey Family Foundation; Ethan J. Litman; Mary McDermid; the Rehael Fund of the Minneapolis Foundation; Deborah Reynolds; Schwegman, Lundberg, Woessner, P.A.; John Sjoberg; Charles Steffey and Suzannah Martin; Jeffrey Sugerman; the Archie D. & Bertha H. Walker Foundation; Stu Wilson and Mel Barker; the Woessner Freeman Family Foundation in memory of David Hilton; and many other generous individual donors.

To you and our many readers across the country, we send our thanks for your continuing support.